The Official
CHELSEA FC
Annual 2014

Written by David Antill, Richard Godden, James Sugrue and Dominic Bliss
Thanks to Adam Daniell

Designed by Brian Thomson

A Grange Publication

© 2013. Published by Grange Communications Ltd., Edinburgh, under licence from Chelsea FC Merchandising Limited. www.chelseafc.com. Printed in the EU.

Photography © Chelsea FC, Press Association, Action Images and Shutterstock

ISBN: 978-1-908925-39-8

£7.99

HELLO GEEZERS!

I hope you enjoyed the last year, when we won another new trophy – the UEFA Europa League – for our amazing club.

You will definitely enjoy your Chelsea Annual this year. We have some incredible features for you, about all your favourite Blues players and also some of the great moments in our history. We always play with great pride for our club and I hope you like watching us as much as we like playing. You are the best supporters in the world. Keep singing for us and keep supporting us!

Come on you Blues!

David Luiz

HONOURS LIST

LEAGUE TITLES: FOUR
1954/55, 2004/05, 2005/06, 2009/10

FA CUPS: SEVEN
1969/70, 1996/97, 1999/00, 2006/07,
2008/09, 2009/10, 2011/12

LEAGUE CUPS: FOUR
1964/65, 1997/98, 2004/05, 2006/07

UEFA CHAMPIONS LEAGUE: ONE
2011/12

UEFA EUROPA LEAGUE: ONE
2012/13

EUROPEAN CUP WINNERS' CUP: TWO
1970/71, 1997/98

UEFA SUPER CUP: ONE
1998

COMMUNITY SHIELDS: FOUR
1955, 2000, 2005, 2009

FA YOUTH CUPS: FOUR
1959/60, 1960/61, 2009/10, 2011/12

CONTENTS

STORY OF THE SEASON

Chelsea made it back-to-back European triumphs by lifting the UEFA Europa League trophy at the end of a season in which we played an incredible 69 games. Here's how it all unfolded...

Chelsea enjoyed a dream start to the Barclays Premier League season, scoring twice in the opening seven minutes to defeat Wigan Athletic. Eden Hazard set up both goals with his silky skills and it meant the Blues continued our record of not being defeated on the opening day since 1998, having won 12 and drawn twice since losing to Coventry City.

Our defence of the UEFA Champions League began with a 2-2 draw against Juventus, a game that will be remembered for two spectacular goals by Oscar. But the less said about his celebration with David Luiz, the better!

The Blues beat both of north London's top clubs, Arsenal and Tottenham Hotspur, on their own grounds – which meant we had started the season with seven wins from our first eight Premier League games. Gary Cahill's worldie against Spurs was almost as good as Oscar's Goal of the Season against Juventus!

There were plenty of tricks in the Halloween treat served up by Chelsea and Manchester United in the Capital One Cup! The Blues had to come from behind on no less than three occasions – including a last-minute penalty from Eden Hazard – but eventually won 5-4 after extra-time.

The fans in Japan were over the moon to see Chelsea arrive in the country to play in the FIFA Club World Cup, which only the best team in Europe gets to compete in each year! Unfortunately, Brazilian side Corinthians were too strong for us in the final.

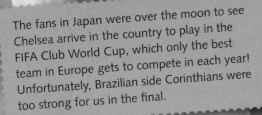

Fernando Torres was one of seven different goalscorers for Chelsea as the Blues gave supporters an early Christmas present by equalling our biggest-ever Premier League win! Aston Villa were on the receiving end as we ran up an 8-0 scoreline.

Petr Cech became the first foreign player to appear in 400 games for Chelsea, but Frank Lampard was the hero with two goals as we became the first, and only, team to beat Everton at Goodison Park in the 2012/13 Premier League season.

Welcome to Chelsea! Demba Ba made his debut against Southampton in the Blues' first game of our FA Cup defence, and he scored two goals in a 5-1 win to show the fans just what he was capable of.

Stoke City's Jon Walters should have been wearing a Chelsea shirt when we travelled to the Britannia Stadium! The Potters lost 4-0 – the first time they had been beaten at home in 17 Premier League games – with Walters scoring two own goals AND missing a penalty. Thanks, Jon!

Chelsea finished just two points above Arsenal, so it certainly helped that we won home and away against the Gunners in 2012/13. The second victory came with the snow falling in January, thanks to a brilliant goal by Juan Mata and Frank Lampard's penalty.

The Blues were knocked out of the UEFA Champions League in the group stage, but that just meant we dropped into the UEFA Europa League. Our first-ever game in the competition came against Sparta Prague, which was one of Petr Cech's first clubs, and Oscar scored a great goal just 30 seconds after coming off the bench!

It was fitting that Frank Lampard's 200th goal should come against West Ham United, the club he left in 2001 to join the Blues. Eden Hazard grabbed our other goal in a 2-0 win, which took us back up to third place.

Demba Ba was no fool on 1 April, as the Senegalese striker scored an absolute worldie to beat Manchester United in the FA Cup! Unfortunately, our hold on the trophy came to an end in the semi-finals when Manchester City beat us at Wembley.

Fernando Torres was dubbed "Zorres" by Chelsea fans – after the Mask of Zorro – following his two sublime goals against Rubin Kazan which helped us reach the semi-finals of the UEFA Europa League.

The short trip across west London was made all the more memorable by David Luiz's stunning 35-yard strike which helped beat Fulham. It was almost forgotten that John Terry scored twice!

David Luiz scored in both legs of our UEFA Europa League semi-final with Basel, but so too did Victor Moses. The Nigerian speedster, who loves to celebrate with a back-flip, netted four goals in total in his first season competing in the UEFA Europa League.

Juan Mata's goal gave us a win over champions Manchester United at Old Trafford, moving the Blues a step closer to UEFA Champions League qualification. We've won more games and taken more points off United at their home ground than any other team in Premier League history!

Remember the date of 11 May 2013 as Super Frank became Chelsea's record goalscorer. What's more, his goals beat Aston Villa to secure our place in the top four!

The Blues made history against Benfica, becoming the first side to win the UEFA Champions League and then the UEFA Europa League in consecutive seasons. Fernando Torres grabbed our first, but it took a last-minute header from Branislav "The Beast" Ivanovic to bring home the trophy. Up the Blues!

MOURINHO
MAKES HAPPY RETURN

One of the best pieces of news for Blues fans came early in summer 2013 when the club announced that José Mourinho would be returning as first-team manager.

Mourinho previously took charge at Chelsea between 2004 and 2007, when he led us to two Premier League titles, an FA Cup and two League Cups.

Since he has been away, the 50-year-old has managed Italian side Inter and Spanish club Real Madrid, where he achieved further success.

He won Serie A twice in two years and the UEFA Champions League with Inter, before winning La Liga and the Copa Del Rey (Spain's equivalent of the Premier League and FA Cup) with Real. He was also named FIFA World Coach of the Year for 2010 and has won Manager of the Season honours in Portugal, England and Italy.

"If I had to describe myself I would describe myself as a very happy person," he said after signing a four-year contract. "It's the first time I've arrived at a club where I already love the club.

"It's a young squad with a lot of talent and they need stability, which I hope I can give them. I'm very confident I can help the team and help the boys develop."

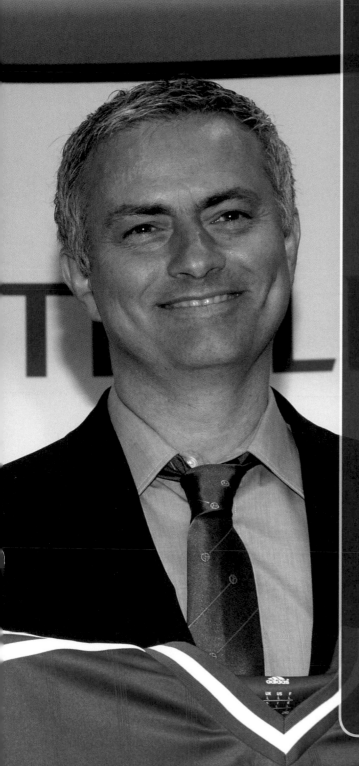

José Mourinho factfile:

Date of birth: 26 January 1963

Place of birth: Setúbal, Portugal

Previous clubs: Benfica, União de Leiria, Porto, Chelsea, Inter, Real Madrid

Managerial honours

Porto (2002–2004)
2 x Primeira Liga (2002/03, 2003/04); Taça de Portugal (2002/03); Supertaça Cândido de Oliveira (2003); UEFA Cup (2002/03); UEFA Champions League (2003/04)

Chelsea (2004–2007)
2 x Premier League (2004/05, 2005/06); FA Cup (2006/07); 2 x League Cup (2004/05, 2006/07); FA Community Shield (2005)

Inter (2008–2010)
2 x Serie A (2008/09, 2009/10); Supercoppa Italiana (2008); Coppa Italia (2009/10); UEFA Champions League (2009/10)

Real Madrid (2010–2013)
Copa Del Rey (2010/11); La Liga (2011/12); Supercopa de España (2012)

Did you know?

In the first season under Mourinho's management – 2004/05 – the Blues won two trophies: the League Cup and the Premier League. It was the first time we were crowned champions in 50 years and we topped the division with a record 95 points and a record low of just 15 goals conceded in 38 games.

Chelsea did not lose a league game at Stamford Bridge during Mourinho's first spell in charge. We won 46 and drew 14.

PLAYER PROFILES

Goalkeepers

1 PETR CECH

Born: Plzen, Czech Republic, 20.05.1982
Height: 1.96m
Signed from: Rennes (July 2004)
Appearances: 432
Clean sheets: 198

Did You Know? After taking to the field in Chelsea's 2-1 win over Everton in December 2012, Petr became the first foreign player to appear in 400 matches for the Blues.

40 HENRIQUE HILARIO

Born: Sao Pedro da Cova, Portugal, 21.10.1975
Height: 1.89m
Signed from: CD Nacional (May 2006)
Appearances: 39
Clean sheets: 18

Did You Know? Known as "H" by his team-mates, the Portuguese goalkeeper made his debut for the club against Barcelona in October 2006. The Blues won the game 1-0.

46 JAMAL BLACKMAN

Born: Croydon, England, 27.10.1993
Height: 1.99m
Turned pro: July 2011
Appearances: 0
Clean sheets: 0

Did You Know? Jamal played in every round of the 2011/12 FA Youth Cup as the Blues lifted the trophy for a second time in three seasons.

23 MARK SCHWARZER

Born: Sydney, Australia, 06.10.1972

Height: 1.96m

Signed from: Free transfer (July 2013)

Appearances: 0

Clean sheets: 0

Did You Know? Mark used to play for our west-London neighbours Fulham and he played in the UEFA Europa League final for the Whites in 2010.

Defenders

28 CESAR AZPILICUETA

Born: Pamplona, Spain, 28.08.1989

Height: 1.78m

Signed from: Marseille (August 2012)

Appearances: 48

Goals: 0

Did You Know? Don't worry if you can't pronounce his surname properly – just follow the lead of the Chelsea fans, who have nicknamed him "Dave"!

34 RYAN BERTRAND

Born: Southwark, England, 05.08.1989

Height: 1.79m

Turned pro: August 2006

Appearances: 54

Goals: 2

Did You Know? Ryan made his UEFA Champions League debut in the 2012 final as the Blues defeated Bayern Munich to be crowned champions of Europe.

3 ASHLEY COLE

Born: Stepney, England, 20.12.1980

Height: 1.76m

Signed from: Arsenal (August 2006)

Appearances: 312

Goals: 7

Did You Know? Ash has won the FA Cup seven times, which is more than any other player in the history of the competition.

Defenders (cont)

24 GARY CAHILL

Born: Sheffield, England, 19.12.1985

Height: 1.93m

Signed from: Bolton Wanderers (January 2012)

Appearances: 64

Goals: 8

Did You Know? Gaz scored a wonder goal against Spurs last season, but it wasn't his favourite strike of the season – he gave that honour to fellow centre-back David Luiz for his sublime effort against Basel!

2 BRANISLAV IVANOVIC

Born: Sremska Mitrovica, Serbia, 22.02.1984

Height: 1.85m

Signed from: Lokomotiv Moscow (January 2008)

Appearances: 219

Goals: 22

Did You Know? When Manchester United's Nemanja Vidic retired from international football in 2011, Brana took on the captain's armband for Serbia.

33 TOMAS KALAS

Born: Olomouc, Czech Republic, 15.05.1993

Height: 1.84m

Signed from: Sigma Olomouc (January 2011)

Appearances: 0

Goals: 0

Did You Know? Tomas won the Czech Republic Young Player of the Year award in 2013 while on loan at Vitesse Arnhem.

4 DAVID LUIZ

Born: Diadema, Brazil, 22.04.1987

Height: 1.89m

Signed from: Benfica (January 2011)

Appearances: 109

Goals: 12

Did You Know? If he could choose to be any superhero, David Luiz would be Spiderman so he could "help the people".

26 JOHN TERRY

Born: Barking, England, 07.12.1980

Height: 1.87m

Turned pro: March 1998

Appearances: 574

Goals: 55

Did You Know? JT is the only defender in the history of Chelsea Football Club to score more than 50 goals in a Blue shirt.

Midfielders

15 KEVIN DE BRUYNE

Born: Ghent, Belgium, 28.06.1991

Height: 1.80m

Signed from: Genk (January 2012)

Appearances: 0

Goals: 0

Did You Know? Kevin's mum was born in Ealing, which is less than 10 miles away from Stamford Bridge!

5 MICHAEL ESSIEN

Born: Accra, Ghana, 03.12.1982

Height: 1.77m

Signed from: Lyon (August 2005)

Appearances: 247

Goals: 25

Did You Know? As well as being named Chelsea Player of the Year in 2007, Michael has also won our Goal of the Season award on two occasions.

17 EDEN HAZARD

Born: La Louvière, Belgium, 07.01.1991

Height: 1.73m

Signed from: Lille (July 2012)

Appearances: 62

Goals: 13

Did You Know? Eden was nominated for the PFA Player and Young Player of the Year awards in 2012/13, as well as being named in the Team of the Season.

Midfielders (cont)

8 FRANK LAMPARD

Born: Romford, England, 20.06.1978

Height: 1.84m

Signed from: West Ham (June 2001)

Appearances: 608

Goals: 203

Did You Know? Lamps is one of three men to have appeared in over 600 games for Chelsea, the others being Ron Harris and Peter Bonetti, who played for the Blues in the 1970s.

10 JUAN MATA

Born: Burgos, Spain, 28.04.1988

Height: 1.72m

Signed from: Valencia (August 2011)

Appearances: 118

Goals: 32

Did You Know? Juan was one of four players to hit double figures for both goals (12) and assists (12) in the 2012/13 Premier League season.

12 JOHN OBI MIKEL

Born: Jos, Nigeria, 22.04.1987

Height: 1.88m

Signed from: Lyn Oslo (June 2006)

Appearances: 277

Goals: 2

Did You Know? Mikel is yet to score a Premier League goal for Chelsea in seven seasons – his only goals for the Blues came in the FA Cup in 2007.

11 OSCAR

Born: Americana, Brazil, 09.09.1991

Height: 1.79m

Signed from: Internacional (July 2012)

Appearances: 64

Goals: 12

Did You Know? Despite only playing six matches, Oscar finished as the sixth leading scorer in the 2012/13 UEFA Champions League after netting five times.

7 RAMIRES

Born: Barra do Pirai, Brazil, 24.03.1987

Height: 1.80m

Signed from: Benfica (August 2010)

Appearances: 150

Goals: 23

Did You Know? Ramires won Chelsea's Goal of the Year award in each of his first two seasons at the club.

16 MARCO VAN GINKEL

Born: Amersfoort, Netherlands, 01.12.1992

Height: 1.86m

Signed from: Vitesse Arnhem (July 2013)

Appearances: 0

Goals: 0

Did You Know? Marco was recently named Dutch Talent of the Year, joining a list which includes former Chelsea players Arjen Robben, Salomon Kalou and Boudewijn Zenden.

22 WILLIAN

Born: Ribeirão Pires, Brazil, 09.08.1988

Height: 1.75m

Signed from: Anzhi Makhachkala (August 2013)

Appearances: 0

Goals: 0

Did You Know? Willian scored twice for Shakhtar Donetsk at Stamford Bridge in 2012, although his side were eventually beaten 3-2.

19 DEMBA BA

Born: Sèvres, France, 25.05.1985

Height: 1.89m

Signed from: Newcastle United (January 2013)

Appearances: 22

Goals: 6

Did You Know? Despite only spending the first half of the season at St James' Park, Demba finished as Newcastle United's top Premier League goalscorer in 2012/13.

29 SAMUEL ETO'O

Born: Nkon, Cameroon, 10.03.1981

Height: 1.80m

Signed from: Anzhi Makhachkala (August 2013)

Appearances: 0

Goals: 0

Did You Know? Eto'o made his debut for the Cameroon national team shortly before his 16th birthday!

14 ANDRE SCHURRLE

Born: Lugwigshafen, Germany, 06.11.1990

Height: 1.83m

Signed from: Bayer Leverkusen (June 2013)

Appearances: 0

Goals: 0

Did You Know? When he was a kid, Andre had a Chelsea shirt with "Lampard" on the back of it!

9 FERNANDO TORRES

Born: Madrid, Spain, 20.03.1984

Height: 1.86m

Signed from: Liverpool (January 2011)

Appearances: 131

Goals: 34

Did You Know? After the Blues beat Benfica in Amsterdam, Fernando was – for 10 days – simultaneously a holder of the UEFA Europa League, UEFA Champions League, World Cup and European Championship!

The Three Amigos!

Chelsea's creative attacking play made us one of the most entertaining teams in the Premier League last season and at the hub of that work, operating between the lines of midfield and attack, were three wonderfully gifted playmakers...

Eden Hazard In his first season in English football, Eden Hazard was shorlisted for both the PFA Player of the Year and Young Player of the Year awards, paying testament to the form he showed in Chelsea colours. There was a great deal of excitement surrounding the Belgian when he arrived at Stamford Bridge and his incredible speed, amazing skills and great confidence meant that defenders quite simply ran scared when they saw him coming!

Juan Mata The oldest of the "Three Amigos", Juan Mata is also the only one who was playing his second season in 2012/13, having already clinched the club's Player of the Year award in his first campaign. He repeated the feat in his follow-up season and his performances just seem to get better and better. Mata is blessed with great vision – he sees a pass where others do not – and that is how he creates so many goals. He is not bad at taking the chances that his team-mates make for him, either, as his return of 20 goals last season proved.

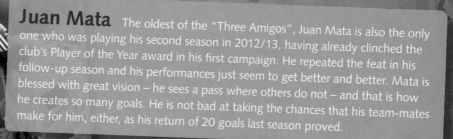

Oscar Scorer of Chelsea's official Goal of the Season in 2012/13 for his amazing long-range strike against Juventus in the Champions League group stage, Oscar has shown great maturity for such a young man in his first season in England. His technical ability is second-to-none and he uses his body well to shield the ball and hold off much bigger and stronger players than himself. Oscar is just like Mata and Hazard in that he can play either as a winger or in the middle of the three creative players who operate behind the striker at Chelsea. His early promise suggests there is much more to come from this boy from Brazil.

LAMPARD & TAMBLING:
HOTSHOTS!

Before the final game of the 2012/13 campaign at Stamford Bridge last season, there was an opportunity for supporters to pay tribute to the two greatest goalscorers in the history of Chelsea. Bobby Tambling, who scored 202 goals for the Blues between 1959 and 1970, came onto the pitch to hand a golden boot trophy to Frank Lampard, after his 202nd and 203rd goals for the club had come a week earlier against Aston Villa. It made Chelsea's vice-captain the highest scorer of all time for the club.

LEGENDARY LAMPARD

Frank's goals total came over a remarkable 12 seasons at the club and he scored 20 goals or more in five of those seasons. That would be a special achievement for any player, but don't forget that Lampard is a midfielder! His best goals return came in 2009/10, when Chelsea won the League and FA Cup Double – he scored 27 goals that season, six more than in his second-best campaign.

Arguably his most famous goals came in the same game, when he scored twice as Chelsea sealed their first ever Premier League title by winning 2-0 at Bolton in April 2005.

VILLANS VANQUISHED

At the end of last season, Lampard had 203 goals and it was fitting that the two he scored to equal, and then break, Tambling's record had come against Aston Villa. At the time he had scored more goals against them than any other team – 14 of his goals total had gone into the Villa net over the years.

They must be sick of the sight of him!

BOBBY DAZZLER

The man Lampard overtook to top the all-time Chelsea scorers' charts, Bobby Tambling, had been at the top of the pile for 43 years but he said he was delighted to see Frank break his record. "If you take what Frank has done personally and then add in what Chelsea have done as a team in the last 10 years, he must surely go down not just as one of the greats but probably the greatest player Chelsea has had," he said.

A true gentleman.

TOP ALL-TIME SCORERS*

Frank Lampard 203

Bobby Tambling 202

Kerry Dixon
(shown right) 193

Didier Drogba 157

Roy Bentley 150

Peter Osgood 150

Jimmy Greaves 132

George Mills 125

George Hilsdon 108

*Figures correct as of the start of the 2013/14 Barclays Premier League season.

GOALKEEPER
FUN
& GAMES!!!

THEY SAY YOU HAVE TO BE A BIT CRAZY TO BE A GOALKEEPER, AND CHELSEA'S NET MINDERS CERTAINLY LIKE TO DO THINGS A BIT DIFFERENTLY.

Spending so much time together on and off the training pitch, they are obviously good friends, and their unique training methods usually bring a smile to their team-mates' faces.

(RIGHT) Goalkeeping and basketball share a lot of skills, making it an obvious way for the Blues' stoppers to practice their handling. Even wearing his gloves Jamal Blackman impressed, with one slam-dunk earning the instant respect of his team-mates.

(BELOW) The team photograph always gets spirits high among the squad as a new season begins. Henrique Hilario might have got a little carried away, though. He decided to take on the role of cameraman, before being reminded that he was supposed to be in the photo!

Whenever the goalkeepers finish training with one of their unusual games, there is always a punishment for the losers. However, when one forfeit involved a series of forward rolls, Blackman got so dizzy that even Hilario's help couldn't get him back to his feet!

Blackman isn't the only goalkeeper with a hidden skill away from the football pitch. As well as being Chelsea's No1, Petr Cech is also a pretty handy drummer and took the chance to show off his musical talent during our post-season tour of the USA.

As a big sports fan, it is no surprise that Cech caught Olympic fever when the Games came to the capital. When swimmer Chad le Clos visited our Cobham training ground, Cech was quick to grab a photo with the South African, along with the gold and silver medals he won at London 2012.

AFRICAN CHAMPIONS

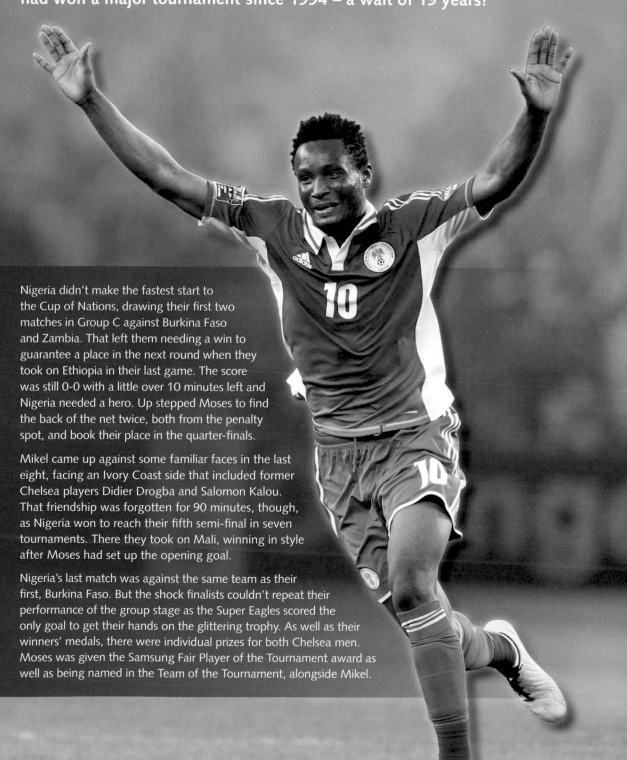

Chelsea won the UEFA Europa League in 2012/13, but there was an extra bit of silverware for John Obi Mikel and Victor Moses last season. Both players helped Nigeria to be crowned kings of their continent by winning the Africa Cup of Nations at the start of the year. The Super Eagles lifted the trophy for the third time in South Africa, but it was the first time they had won a major tournament since 1994 – a wait of 19 years!

Nigeria didn't make the fastest start to the Cup of Nations, drawing their first two matches in Group C against Burkina Faso and Zambia. That left them needing a win to guarantee a place in the next round when they took on Ethiopia in their last game. The score was still 0-0 with a little over 10 minutes left and Nigeria needed a hero. Up stepped Moses to find the back of the net twice, both from the penalty spot, and book their place in the quarter-finals.

Mikel came up against some familiar faces in the last eight, facing an Ivory Coast side that included former Chelsea players Didier Drogba and Salomon Kalou. That friendship was forgotten for 90 minutes, though, as Nigeria won to reach their fifth semi-final in seven tournaments. There they took on Mali, winning in style after Moses had set up the opening goal.

Nigeria's last match was against the same team as their first, Burkina Faso. But the shock finalists couldn't repeat their performance of the group stage as the Super Eagles scored the only goal to get their hands on the glittering trophy. As well as their winners' medals, there were individual prizes for both Chelsea men. Moses was given the Samsung Fair Player of the Tournament award as well as being named in the Team of the Tournament, alongside Mikel.

UEFA EUROPA LEAGUE SPECIAL

(Top) Celebration time for the Blues after our second European triumph in as many seasons.

(Left) Stamford the Lion enjoys the atmosphere at the Amsterdam ArenA.

(Bottom, left) Frank Lampard celebrates our last-ditch winner.

(Below) Petr Cech gets his hands on yet another piece of silverware.

(Left) Branislav Ivanovic heads a dramatic late winner for the Blues.

(Below) Goalscorers Fernando Torres and Branislav Ivanovic proudly show off the UEFA Europa League trophy.

BRAZIL AT THE BRIDGE

IN March 2013, Stamford Bridge hosted an international match for the first time since 1946, and it was the first-ever time two foreign national teams had played each other at the stadium. The news that Brazil would take on Russia got Chelsea's own Brazilian trio David Luiz, Ramires and Oscar especially excited, parading their country's flag around the pitch to celebrate.

Blues David Luiz and Oscar both took their place in the Selecao's starting line-up, getting a great reception from both the Chelsea and Brazil fans in the crowd. However, Ramires missed out on the game because of an injury.

There was a real party atmosphere at the Bridge on the day of the game, as the Brazil fans and even some traditional Samba dancers brought the carnival spirit from Rio de Janeiro to west London.

The match finished in 1-1 draw, with Fred heading a late equaliser for Brazil after Victor Fayzulin had put Russia ahead in the second half.

It wasn't just current Chelsea players on show, as former player Yury Zhirkov returned with Russia, to the stadium where he won the Premier League and FA Cup during two seasons with the Blues between 2009 and 2011.

it's blue,
what else matters?

When Chelsea's official kit supplier and sponsor adidas announced that our new kit for the 2013/14 season would be available to pre-order before it was revealed, they needed a campaign to catch people's eye.

What they came up with certainly grabbed attention, thanks to the dedication of the Blues' first-team squad.

The players arrived at the adidas studio for the photo shoot ready to show the lengths they will go to for Chelsea, covering themselves in blue paint in a number of interesting ways for the "it's blue, what else matters?" teaser campaign.

MATA (main pic)

Juan Mata definitely seemed to be enjoying making a mess, as two of the adidas crew at the photo shoot threw bucket after bucket of paint at him, but the Spaniard just kept asking for more!

CAHILL (above)

Things were starting to get a bit more creative by the time it was Gary Cahill's turn to step out into the spotlight. No effort was spared as adidas created a blue waterfall for the centre-back to walk through.

BA (left)

Probably the most athletic contribution came from striker Demba Ba. The Senegalese international showed off his flawless technique with a few aerial volleys, splattering the screens with paint in the process.

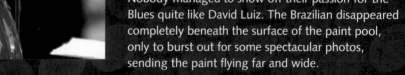

LUIZ (above)

Nobody managed to show off their passion for the Blues quite like David Luiz. The Brazilian disappeared completely beneath the surface of the paint pool, only to burst out for some spectacular photos, sending the paint flying far and wide.

TORRES (above)

Fernando Torres kept things fairly simple, being covered from head to toe using a nice old-fashioned bucket, before replicating his familiar knee-slide goal celebration.

TERRY (right)

Captain John Terry led by example as always, jumping straight into a bath of paint despite the cold. He let himself fall backwards into the giant pool, proving that Chelsea always make waves, and putting those watching at risk of being covered in paint too.

10 YEARS OF ROMAN ABRAMOVICH

On 1 July, 2013, Chelsea celebrated 10 years of Roman Abramovich's ownership of the club and what a decade it has been for the club! With 13 pieces of major silverware added to the trophy cabinet, including three Premier League titles and a UEFA Champions League title, this has been the most successful period in our history. Let's take a look at 10 years of fantastic achievements...

FIRST IMPACT

With Roman Abramovich's investment fuelling the club, the first season of his ownership – 2003/04 – was one of instant progress at Chelsea. The arrivals of superstars like Claude Makelele, Hernan Crespo, Damien Duff and Joe Cole, among several other big names, boosted Claudio Ranieri's squad into a new stratosphere and the team responded with a second-place finish in the Premier League, while also reaching the semi-finals of the UEFA Champions League. Not bad!

CHAMPIONS OF ENGLAND!

The 2004/05 campaign was one of the most memorable in the club's history as José Mourinho arrived to take charge of the team and managed Chelsea to their first league title in 50 years! It was also the year that several legends arrived, including Petr Cech, Didier Drogba, Ricardo Carvalho, Paulo Ferreira and Arjen Robben. After a dominant season, Frank Lampard was voted Footballer of the Year and JT was voted PFA Player of the Year as the club also lifted the League Cup. Incredibly, the club's first Premier League success also saw us finish with 95 points, a record that still stands!

COLLECTING TROPHIES

The triumphs of 2004/05 sent the team into overdrive as they started collecting trophies! The next year, with the team boosted by the arrival of Michael Essien and several other big signings, Chelsea won the Premier League again. They followed that with a League Cup and FA Cup double in 2006/07, after Ashley Cole, Michael Ballack, Andriy Shevchenko, John Obi Mikel and Salomon Kalou had signed. Then, in 2007/08, Chelsea reached their first-ever UEFA Champions League Final in 2008, with Avram Grant as manager – defeat to Manchester United on penalties left us with something to chase, however!

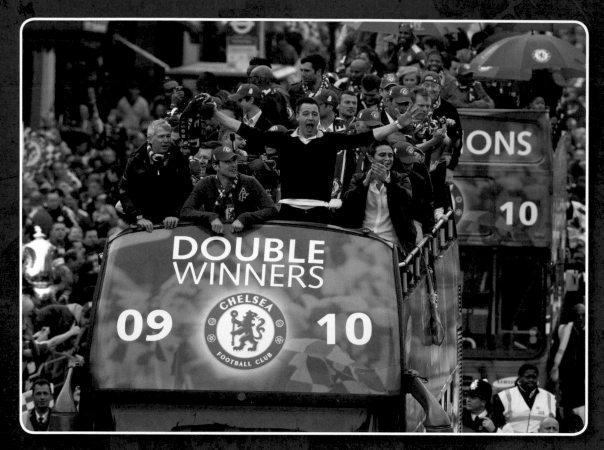

DOUBLE WINNERS

Although each of the domestic trophies had made their way to Stamford Bridge by 2009, the season that followed would see Chelsea, now under the management of Carlo Ancelotti, win the League and FA Cup Double for the first time. Since the

UEFA Champions League Final in 2008, Luiz Felipe Scolari and Guus Hiddink had taken charge of the team, with Hiddink lifting the FA Cup in 2009, but Ancelotti brought the Premier League title back to west London in 2010. His team scored a league record 103 goals and also won the FA Cup for a second consecutive season.

CHAMPIONS OF EUROPE

The biggest piece of silverware in club football was added to Chelsea's collection of trophies in 2012, as Roman Abramovich's successful era was adorned with a first European triumph. After memorable victories over Napoli, Benfica and reigning champions Barcelona, we met Bayern Munich in the final, in their own stadium. Despite going a goal behind, a header by Didier Drogba and an incredible Petr Cech penalty save from former team-mate Arjen Robben, took the game to a penalty shoot-out, where Cech continued to frustrate Bayern, allowing Drogba to step up and score the winning penalty with his last-ever kick in a Chelsea shirt. The Blues were Champions of Europe and they celebrated with an open-top bus tour.

OFF THE PITCH

There have been so many superstars and trophy triumphs since Roman Abramovich bought the club in 2003 that it is hard to remember them all! However, the impact of his ownership has also been felt off the pitch. Chelsea now have one of the best training facilities in world football at Cobham, and an Academy to match it, producing young talent that has won the FA Youth Cup twice in the last four years. The club launched our own charity – the Chelsea Foundation – and embraced the Blues' heritage more than ever before by introducing a more traditional badge. The Past Players' Trust was set up to support the club's former heroes and to keep in touch with everyone who has contributed to the great history of Chelsea. It means we never lose sight of the men who made our club what it is today.

NOW AND NEXT

Last season saw Chelsea – with a team of exciting young talent, mixed with experienced legends – lift the UEFA Europa League trophy, with goals from Fernando Torres and Branislav Ivanovic overpowering Benfica. We also witnessed Frank Lampard become the club's all-time top goalscorer, with his 203rd goal for Chelsea. It was a strong end to the campaign and, with some incredible young talent in the side, the likes of David Luiz, Oscar, Juan Mata and Eden Hazard – among several others – the future is bright.

INTERNATIONAL CENTURIONS

Three Chelsea players brought up a century of international appearances during the 2012/13 season.

We pay tribute to the trio who have served their country with distinction over the years...

PETR CECH

As Petr Cech pointed out, "It's harder to get to 100 caps as a goalkeeper – there is only one place in the team for you, so if you're not the No1 for a long time then you cannot reach this." After debuting in 2002, that's exactly what he has done, keeping his place in the team ever since, to close-to-within touching distance of his country's all-time leading appearance maker. That man is Karel Poborsky, who you might remember from his time at Manchester United and the shocking hair-do he had! Big Pete certainly has the advantage in the style stakes...

ASHLEY COLE

It took Ashley Cole just four appearances for England's Under-21s side to show he was ready for international football in 2001 against Albania. Twelve years later, he was being presented with a golden cap to mark his achievement of reaching 100 caps, which has only been done by six other players – although Frank Lampard might be next! Not only did Ash start each of those 100 appearances, 22 of them came at international tournaments, which is a record for England. He has also been capped more times for the Three Lions than any other full-back. Not bad, Ash!

FERNANDO TORRES

Fernando Torres was the first Blues star to celebrate his century, which came shortly after he was awarded the Golden Boot for finishing as the top scorer at Euro 2012. He was on target in the final against Italy, just as he had been four years earlier when Spain beat Germany – and no Spanish player has scored more goals at European Championships than El Nino! His country also won the World Cup in 2010, proving that they are the dominant side in world football. What's their secret? As our picture of Nando from 10 years ago shows, he hasn't aged a bit!

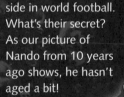

SPOT THE BALL

Can you work out which is the real ball in the picture below?

Answer on Page 61

WORDSEARCH

Frank Lampard became our all-time highest scorer in 2013, but can you find the names of our No8 and the rest of the top 20 in the grid below? They can go upwards, downwards or diagonally in any direction. Good luck!

```
D L Z F Z W Q T C G S E V A E R G
R L Q K M K B W L A M P A R D K Q
O A M A H G N I T T I H W L C N K
G D Y K Z O L A N J H P Y K N I R
B N B R I D G E S Q N E K O V A T
A I K N X F T Z E W L Q D D Z B P
M T M I H K N S R T T S Z K P L B
I L B W L N I Y N Z L L G L P E L
L M W D M W E E Y I N G G M N S K
L Q M L V C B S H G A P B M N S G
S H P A K O N J N L N D R P G A F
Z N Y B S C X I L H K I I M Z H M
G J J G B T R A C V O B L X G N W
G Z O K W M C R J H L J G B O Q P
T O M C C H F T N T O N D T M N D
D E C N E P S Z H Q Q L D U Y A D
X R K R W N X Y M Z P N F Q G Y T
```

BALDWIN
BENTLEY
BRIDGES
DIXON
DROGBA

GALLACHER
GREAVES
GUDJOHNSEN
HASSELBAINK
HILSDON

LAMPARD
MCNICHOL
MILLS
OSGOOD
SPENCE

TAMBLING
TINDALL
WHITTINGHAM
WISE
ZOLA

Answers on Page 61

41

CHELSEA ACADEMY

2012/13 was another season to remember for the Academy with two major finals to reflect on...

UP FOR THE YOUTH CUP

After winning the FA Youth Cup last season, youth-team manager Adi Viveash's Under-18s reached the final again this year, with some fantastic performances along the way.

Chelsea dominated possession and territory for much of the two-legged final against Norwich City but they failed to make their chances count and were caught out by some rapid counterattacking. In the end, the young Blues suffered a 4-2 aggregate defeat, but they did the club proud once again, while a combined total of more than 39,000 people watched the two legs.

"We hoped for a different ending, but hopefully you saw the work that goes into the Academy here on a daily basis through the performances on the pitch," said Viveash, addressing the supporters. "You should feel proud that these kids represent your football club."

Nathan Ake, one of the stars of the run to the final, was missing for the second leg at Stamford Bridge because he was involved with the first-team squad for the latter stages of the season. However, the 18-year-old's six senior appearances in 2012/13 were another triumph for the Academy.

DREAM DEBUT IN EUROPE

Chelsea's Under-19s made their first appearance in the NextGen Series last season, taking on the youth teams from many of Europe's best clubs.

With Under-21s manager Dermot Drummy taking charge of the team, they went all the way to the final of the competition, beating the likes of Ajax, Barcelona, Juventus and Arsenal along the way.

Unfortunately, they fell at the last hurdle, losing 2-0 to Aston Villa in the Italian city of Como, where the semi-finals and final were played.

Lewis Baker, who captained the team in their remarkable run, was voted Player of the Tournament and Islam Feruz ended as joint-top scorer with seven goals.

TEAM KIT QUIRKS!

So you've got the latest Chelsea kit with the name of your favourite Blues star on the back, ready to replicate his skills on the pitch?

But there are still those special finishing touches you need to complete your hero's look...

As a kid, Frank Lampard played in shorts that were too big for him, so he rolled them up at the waist. That habit has stayed with him, but with longer under-shorts to avoid any retro "short-shorts" fashion disasters.

LAMPARD

John Terry favours an old school English kit, with a short-sleeve shirt tucked into his shorts whatever the weather. However, our skipper adds a modern touch with his socks pulled up above the knees. To complete the JT look, a captain's armband is a must.

TERRY

CECH

When copying Petr Cech most fans opt for just the head-guard and a pair of goalkeeping gloves. A tight-fitting shirt tucked in at the shorts is also required. You don't need a loose shirt getting in the way at the vital moment!

John Obi Mikel has perfected the art of dealing with the changeable English weather. The midfielder opts for long sleeves with a base layer underneath, simply rolling up the sleeves of one or both tops as the temperature improves.

MIKEL

90 minutes of action can get the sweat flowing, but that's no problem for David Luiz thanks to the sweatbands he wears on both wrists, complete with the Chelsea badge of course.

LUIZ

When winter arrives, it's time to wrap up. Eden Hazard is one of the players to keep warm with matching Blues gloves. These are also needed to complete the Demba Ba, Juan Mata, Victor Moses and Oscar looks.

HAZARD

Ramires is another who favours a pair of Chelsea gloves. However, when you cover as much ground on the pitch as he does, you want to keep things light, sticking with a short-sleeve shirt.

RAMIRES

HOW WELL DO YOU KNOW YOUR BLUES?

Test your knowledge in our Chelsea quiz:

1. How many times have Chelsea won the Premier League?

2. Where is the club's training ground located?

3. Which player in the current Chelsea squad has made the most appearances for the club?

4. And what is the name of our all-time leading appearance-maker?

5. Which country does Eden Hazard play for?

6. Can you name the four Spanish internationals in our squad?

7. What is the name of Chelsea's Chairman?

8. In what year did we last win the FA Cup?

9. Who makes Chelsea's kit?

10. True or false – Chelsea are the second British club to have won all three major UEFA club competitions?

Answers on Page 61

PLAYER BIRTHDAYS – 2014

January

Eden Hazard 7/1/91

February

Branislav Ivanovic 22/2/84

March

Samuel Eto'o 10/3/81
Fernando Torres 20/3/84
Ramires 24/3/87

April

John Obi Mikel 22/4/87
David Luiz 22/4/87
Juan Mata 28/4/88

May

Tomas Kalas 15/5/93
Petr Cech 20/5/82
Demba Ba 25/5/85

June

Frank Lampard 20/6/78
Kevin De Bruyne 28/6/91

August

Ryan Bertrand 5/8/89
Willian 9/8/88
Cesar Azpilicueta 28/8/89

September

Oscar 9/9/91

October

Mark Schwarzer 6/10/72
Henrique Hilario 21/10/75
Jamal Blackman 27/10/93

November

Andre Schurrle 6/11/90

December

Marco van Ginkel 1/12/92
Michael Essien 3/12/82
John Terry 7/12/80
Gary Cahill 19/12/85
Ashley Cole 20/12/80

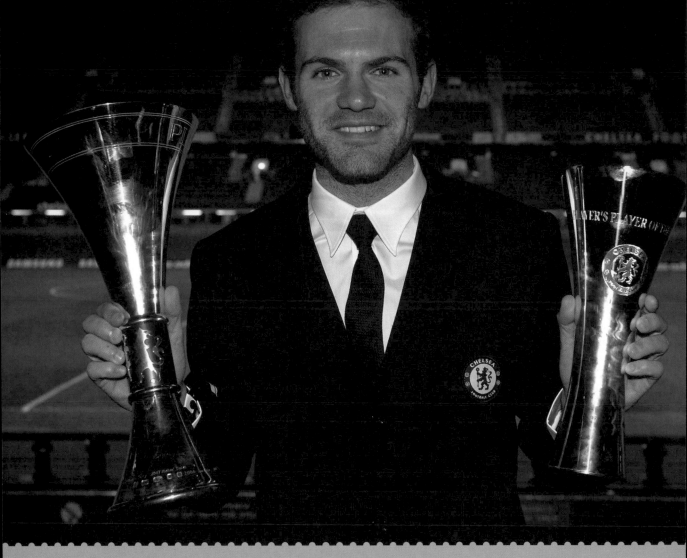

PLAYER OF THE YEAR 2013

DREAM DOUBLE

Juan Mata was the big winner at our 2013 Player of the Year awards.

After being voted by supporters as our best performer at the end of his first season with the club, he once again received the majority of their votes after an impressive 2012/13, when he scored 20 goals and provided 37 assists.

Not only that, but the 25-year-old also got the nod from his team-mates, who voted him Players' Player of the Year.

"I am really, really happy and very proud," said Mata. "It's the best feeling in the world to feel loved by the supporters and my team-mates. It has made my year perfect."

DID YOU KNOW?

Juan Mata became the only Blue to be voted Player of the Year in his first two seasons with the club. He joins John Hollins (1970 and 1971), Ray Wilkins (1976 and 1977) and Frank Lampard (2004 and 2005) as the fourth person to retain the trophy.

PICK THAT ONE OUT

There were some sensational strikes in the shortlist for the 2012/13 Goal of the Season and the award went to one of last summer's new signings, Oscar. The Brazilian international produced a moment of genius in our 2-2 draw against Juventus in September, when he showed a sublime first touch before a stunning shot from outside the area. "It was the best goal of my career so far," said the midfielder. "I was surprised to win but really happy."

Oscar receives applause from his team-mates on his way to collect the Goal of the Season award

Lampard poses with Bobby Tambling after receiving his Special Recognition award

SALUTING A LEGEND

After becoming the club's all-time leading goalscorer, Frank Lampard received a Special Recognition award from the man he overtook, Bobby Tambling. "For Bobby to give me the award and to speak about me like he did, it made me emotional," said Lamps. "I can only say thanks to him for that, it was brilliant." As the only Blue to have been voted by fans as our Player of the Year on three occasions (2004, 2005 and 2009), there's no doubt that Lamps is one of Chelsea's true greats.

ONE TO WATCH

Nathan Ake ended a memorable season by being crowned Young Player of the Year. The Dutch Academy product appeared for both our Under-18s and Under-21s in 2012/13 but also made six first-team appearances, ending the campaign by making his full Premier League debut on the final day against Everton.
"If you'd told me all this would happen a year ago, I wouldn't have believed it," said Ake. "To be involved with this squad is really good for my development and a great experience."

Nathan Ake was voted Young Player of the Year after a season of progress

INSIDER: BEHIND THE SCENES DURING THE SEASON

It's not just on the football pitch that the Chelsea players catch the eye. We take a look back at some of the squad's memorable off-the-field moments over the past year.

When you've just won your second continental trophy in just under a year, you obviously want to celebrate and tell the world. Luckily Oscar was there to help David Luiz on the way back from the UEFA Europa League final in Amsterdam, taking a photo of his Brazilian team-mate with the trophy and his medal to show all his friends and family.

The end of the hard work in training doesn't always mean the players are finished for the day. Some members of the squad are often found staying behind to practice free kicks or even, like Demba Ba and Ashley Cole, to wind down with a game of foot-tennis.

When official club sponsor Samsung asked Fernando Torres and a few others to help them film their new TV advert, the Spanish striker jumped at the chance to show off some of his hidden talents using their household appliances. Our favourite, closely beating Victor Moses' towel folding, was Torres making these delicious cakes.

The players rarely turn down an opportunity to earn bragging rights over their team-mates, so the annual visit of EA Sports to Cobham for a FIFA tournament is always popular. Young goalkeeper Jamal Blackman was the 2012/13 champion, but there was a hint of cheating as David Luiz helped him beat Victor Moses in the semi-finals.

The festive spirit hits professional footballers just like the rest of us. Cesar Azpilicueta, Victor Moses and Eden Hazard all joined in to help the local area enjoy the season, by turning on the Christmas lights at Fulham Broadway, near Stamford Bridge. Hazard even treated the crowd to a few Christmas carols while he was at it, despite Moses trying to save everyone's ears.

When the Chelsea squad arrived at a charity event in London to meet some of their young fans, one competition prize caught the eye of David Luiz and Oscar. The Brazilian duo were so impressed by Chelsea table football that they invited a couple of lucky supporters to be their team-mates.

WORLDWIDE BLUES

As well as being one of the most popular clubs in England, Chelsea are gaining more and more supporters worldwide – no surprise considering all the trophies we have won in recent years!

This means more trips around the globe where we regularly sell out stadiums and attract huge crowds for events off the pitch.

Michael Essien and his team-mates step off the plane after arriving in Washington, DC.

American idols

After the end of the 2012/13 season, we travelled to the United States for two games against Manchester City. Both were exciting matches, with us narrowly losing the first 4-3 in St Louis, before we were beaten in an eight-goal thriller in New York. It wasn't just the Blues players who proved popular with the American fans, with Stamford the Lion also attracting plenty of attention at an open training session.

We also prepared for the 2013/14 season by competing in an eight-team tournament in the US. We joined AC Milan, Inter, Juventus, Real Madrid, Valencia, Everton and LA Galaxy for the Guinness International Champions Cup.

Mascots Stamford the Lion and Bridget the Lioness at the MetLife Stadium in New Jersey.

Petr Cech tests his outfield skills at a soccer clinic against youngsters from Harlem FC.

Left: Andre Schurrle celebrates his goal against AC Milan in the Eastern final of the Guinness International Champions Cup at the MetLife Stadium in New Jersey.

Right: Kevin De Bruyne in action against Real Madrid in the Guinness International Champions Cup final at the Sun Life Stadium in Miami.

Here to Play, Here to Stay…

Chelsea travelled to Asia in July for our fourth pre-season tour in that part of the world in the last decade. After visiting the continent in 2003, 2008 and 2011, our following there has grown massively and the Blues received an incredible reception this summer.

Our first game was against a Singha All-Star team in the Thai capital, Bangkok. We then faced a Malaysia XI in Kuala Lumpur before finishing the trip with a game against an Indonesian All-Star team in Jakarta.

As well as getting some valuable practice matches in ahead of the 2013/14 season, the Blues players attended a number of events along with Chelsea Foundation coaches. As the name of the tour – Here to Play, Here to Stay – suggests, the club will leave a lasting legacy once the team returns home, with our Soccer Schools and Blue Pitches forming a big part of our work to improve football at a grassroots level throughout the year.

Fans at Chelsea v BNI Indonesia All-Stars in Jakarta.

Petr Cech visiting the Blue Pitch in Kuala Lumpur.

Romelu Lukaku celebrates after scoring against BNI Indonesia All-Stars.

John Terry lifts the Singha 80th Anniversary Cup after beating Singha All-Stars in Bangkok.

here to **play** | here to **stay**
asia tour 2013
Thailand | Malaysia | Indonesia

CONFEDERATIONS CUP

David Luiz and Oscar got their hands on another trophy in 2013 by helping Brazil win the Confederations Cup in front of their own fans. The final at the famous Maracana stadium in Rio de Janeiro saw the Samba side beat world and European champions Spain 3-0.

Both Blues started every game of the tournament and had a big part to play in Brazil lifting the trophy in the final. Oscar set up Neymar for their second goal, soon after David Luiz had made an incredible clearance off the line.

Fernando Torres was one of three Chelsea players left disappointed after losing the final with Spain, alongside Juan Mata and Cesar Azpilicueta, but had some consolation in winning the adidas Golden Shoe award for the Confederations Cup's top scorer.

It wasn't all bad news for our Spaniards in Brazil, though, as they also set a competition record by beating Tahiti 10-0 in the group stage, with Torres banging in four goals and Mata also getting on the score sheet.

There was a sixth Chelsea player in action at the Confederations Cup, as John Obi Mikel represented Nigeria. The young Super Eagles team couldn't make it to the semi-final after getting a tough draw, but Mikel came home with at least one happy memory after scoring a rare goal in their game against Uruguay.

MEET THE CHELSEA LADIES

Chelsea Ladies are one of the best sides in the FA Women's Super League, but how much do you really know about the Blues? We bring you the inside scoop...

SOFIA JAKOBSSON
One of Sweden's best players, Sofia joined the Blues in 2013 and scored five times in her first six appearances!

ESTER
Brazilian midfielder Ester was welcomed to the club by David Luiz, Oscar and Ramires!

DUNIA SUSI
Dunia can play at full-back or as a winger. She is part Spanish, but luckily for England she chose to represent the Three Lions at international level!

DID YOU KNOW?

Emma Hayes is the manager of Chelsea Ladies. As well as working in the USA, Emma was at Arsenal when the Gunners became the first, and so far only, English side to win the UEFA Women's Champions League. Her assistant manager is Paul Green, who used to be a professional footballer and once played against David Beckham!

Chelsea reached the Women's FA Cup final for the first time in 2012. Sadly, the Blues were beaten by Birmingham City after a penalty shoot-out.

KYLIE DAVIES

A whole-hearted centre-back, just like JT, Kylie also works as a postwoman. It doesn't matter if she's on the pitch. or off it – she always delivers!

WHEATSHEAF PARK

The Ladies play their games at Wheatsheaf Park, which is also the home ground of Staines Town. Actor and comedian Ralf Little used to play for Staines!

WINNERS
UEFA WOMEN'S CHAMPIONS LEAGUE FINAL 2013

WOLFSBURG PLAYERS CELEBRATE

Stamford Bridge was the venue for the UEFA Women's Champions League final in 2013. Lyon went into the game on a 118-match unbeaten run, but it was German side Wolfsburg who took home the trophy!

The official Chelsea Ladies Twitter page is @ChelseaLFC. Nearly all of the players love to tweet and they will answer any questions you have about women's football.

CHELSEA FC SOCCER SCHOOLS

OPERATING ACROSS LONDON AND THE SOUTH DURING EVERY HOLIDAY PERIOD

JUNIOR MEMBERS
R E C E I V E

15% OFF

WHEN BOOKING ONLINE

For more information visit
chelseafc.com/soccerschools

FOUNDATION

QUIZ ANSWERS

Spot the Ball, Page 40

How well do you know your Blues?, Page 46

1. Three: 2005, 2006 and 2010
2. Cobham, Surrey
3. Frank Lampard
4. Ron "Chopper" Harris
5. Belgium
6. Fernando Torres, Juan Mata, Oriol Romeu and Cesar Azpilicueta
7. Bruce Buck
8. 2012
9. Adidas
10. False – we are the only British club to have done this

Wordsearch, Page 41

D	L	Z	F	Z	W	Q	T	C	G	S	E	V	A	E	R	G
R	L	Q	K	M	K	B	W	L	A	M	P	A	R	D	K	Q
O	A	M	A	H	G	N	I	T	T	I	H	W	L	C	N	K
G	D	Y	K	Z	O	L	A	N	J	H	P	Y	K	N	K	R
B	N	B	R	I	D	G	E	S	Q	N	E	K	O	V	A	T
A	I	K	N	X	F	T	Z	E	W	L	Q	D	D	Z	B	P
M	T	M	I	H	K	N	S	R	T	T	S	Z	K	P	L	B
I	L	B	W	L	N	I	Y	N	Z	L	L	G	L	P	E	L
L	M	W	D	M	W	E	E	Y	I	N	G	G	M	N	S	K
L	Q	M	L	V	C	B	S	H	G	A	P	B	M	N	S	G
S	H	P	A	K	O	N	J	N	L	N	D	R	P	G	A	F
Z	N	Y	B	S	C	X	I	L	H	K	I	I	M	Z	H	M
G	J	J	G	B	T	R	A	C	V	O	B	L	X	G	N	W
G	Z	O	K	W	M	C	R	J	H	L	J	B	O	Q	P	P
T	O	M	C	C	H	F	T	N	T	O	N	D	T	M	N	D
D	E	C	N	E	P	S	Z	H	Q	Q	L	D	U	Y	A	D
X	R	K	R	W	N	X	Y	M	Z	P	N	F	Q	G	Y	T

Where's Stamford?

Can you spot Stamford in the picture below?